Six Knots FOR Everyday Life

by Phil Peterson Sr.

Adventure Publications, Inc.
Cambridge, MN

Edited by Brett Ortler

Cover and book design by Jonathan Norberg

Illustrations by Anthony Hertzel and Jonathan Norberg

PHOTO CREDITS:

WJM Barcelon: 61 **Beverly Bate:** 23 **Steve Bonham:** 44 (bottom right) **Tom Claytor:** 30 (top center), 44 (bottom left) **Tinho Dornellas:** 38 (bottom left) **Dan Downing:** 16, 24 (middle right, bottom center), 30 (top left, bottom row), 38 (top left, middle left, bottom center), 43, 44 (top left, middle left, middle right), 50 (top left, middle left, bottom center), 56 (top center, bottom row), 62 (top center), 72 (bottom), 75 (top) **Stewart M. Green:** 50 (top right), 62 (top right, bottom center) **Mark Lund:** 38 (middle center) **Jonathan Norberg:** 44 (bottom center) **Dale Ortler:** 19, 24 (top left), 44 (top center), 50 (middle center, bottom right), 56 (middle right), 62 (middle right, bottom left, bottom right) **Mickey Panayiotakis:** 38 (middle right) **SDFD:** 38 (bottom right), 44 (middle center) **Joe Siudzinski:** 62 (middle left) **Jason Theriault:** 24 (bottom right) **www.davidbeede.com:** 38 (top center) **www.fleecebymail.biz:** 24 (middle center) **www.thrutheatticdoor.com:** 24 (top center)

10 9 8 7 6 5 4 3 2 1

Published by Adventure Publications, Inc.
820 Cleveland Street S
Cambridge, MN 55008
1-800-678-7006
www.adventurepublications.net

ISBN-13: 978-1-59193-205-5
ISBN-10: 1-59193-205-X

Six Knots FOR Everyday Life

DEDICATION

Knowing how to tie a few good knots will make life easier for everyone. Though I don't consider myself an expert in the large, expansive world of knots, I know my six knots and they have gotten me through life so far. They work well, and I want to share them with you, as I'm confident that these six knots will get you through life too.

Please remember these pages were written for people who want the convenience of knowing a select group of simple knots that will meet most of the needs of everyday life. This book is NOT for those who already consider themselves knot experts. The experts may want to expand their repertoires by referring to one of the many thick, all-inclusive knot manuals that seem to include every knot on the planet. Likewise, I may not have included everyone's favorite knot in this book, but the purpose of this book was to select the smallest number of knots that, in my judgment, are as useful as possible.

My thanks for help and encouragement along the way goes out to all my knot-tying friends who had to put up with me for the last year as I tied them to chairs and tables while explaining the strategies of my six favorite knots. Their arguments, insights, and outright dismissal of my attitude on occasion have resulted in what you now read.

Special thanks go again to the Slabaughs of Adventure Publications, to editor Brett Ortler, designer Jonathan Norberg, Dan Downing (the model whose wrists, hands, and fingers grace the photographs of the six knots), and all who helped along the way.

Grab a piece of rope . . . and go tie something up, down, or to something!

Humbly submitted,
Phil Peterson Sr.

TABLE OF CONTENTS

INTRODUCTION

To enjoy this book, begin by temporarily forgetting the knots you already know. Forget their names. Forget how you have used or misused them and how they have worked or failed. Pretend you know nothing about tying. Also, divest yourself of any ingrained frustrations or lingering doubts about your knot-tying abilities. From now on, your knots will work.

I have sailed and canoed for 60 years on the oceans and rivers of North America. During these adventures, I have played with many knots and knot-tying scenarios. In the end, I feel life would be easier for everyone with a simple system of fewer knots—and more instruction on how and when to use them. To me, it is more important to know a handful of knots well than try to learn hundreds of specialty knots.

When I turned 70, my wife got tired of me lamenting, "Why doesn't someone write a *simple* book on how to tie?" She said, "I'm tired of hearing this. Why don't you do it?" Thus, *Six Knots For Everyday Life*.

This book will show those new to tying how and when to use these six simple knots that will serve them well in virtually any circumstance, from the home front to the great outdoors.

HOW TO USE THIS BOOK

Six Knots is designed to make it simple for you to decide which knot you need for any job, then tie (and untie) that knot as quickly and easily as possible. To accomplish this, the book is divided into several sections.

In this book you'll find information about types of rope, tying aids, advice to help you effectively harness a load, secure knots through locking, and other handy tips.

Each of the knots is covered in its own chapter. Here you'll find in-depth explanations about each knot's recommended uses and easy-to-follow, illustrated step-by-step instructions on how to tie the knot. We'll also cover useful variations.

Finally, look for knot-specific hints and fun facts about each knot. While the first and last chapters of the book provide useful reference material, you can easily tie any of the six knots by opening to the chapter and getting started. There's also a pair of bonus knots for tying monofilament nylon and copolymer lines for fishing or crafting! To this end, the charts on pages 12 through 15 show the six knots' recommended uses, and the page numbers on which you can find them.

DISCLAIMER

The publisher and the author make no representations or warranties as to the suitability, application or use of any of the knots described herein, and the reader must use his or her own judgment in each situation. The publisher and the author specifically disclaim any liability for any injury, damage or loss sustained, directly or indirectly, as a result of the use, application or performance in any situation or setting of any of the knots described in this book.

The six knots in this book are great for everyday life—here are a few suggestions to get you started:

Yard/Garden

Household

Holidays/Celebrations

For the Kids

Sports/On the Lake   page

Moving/Hauling   page

KNOT		USE IT:
Square Knot		At the lake, when crafting, in fashion, when camping, in the garden, in the garage
Slip Knot		In the garage, in the garden, with your pets, on the farm, while camping, around the house
Trucker's Hitch		On the farm, while working, when loading a vehicle, when moving, at the lake, whenever tension is needed
Bowline		At the lake, with your pets, on the farm, in the garden, in the yard, in the garage, when campin
Clove Hitch		With your pets, on the farm, in the garden, around the house, in the laundry room, over the holidays, at the lake
Fisherman's Knot or "Granny Splice"		When paddling, when camping, in the yard, at the lake, when crafting
BONUS KNOT #1: **The Double Figure Eight Loop**		At the lake, when camping, when climbing, around the house, over the holidays, when crafting, when using monofilament
BONUS KNOT #2: **Clinch Knot**		At the lake, over the holidays, around the house when crafting, when using monofilament

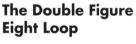

DESCRIPTION

Used to join two ends of the same rope, the Square Knot enjoys worldwide popularity because it is simple, easy to remember, and easy to tie or untie.

A practical, easy-to-tie knot, the Slip Knot is useful on its own and can be incorporated into other knots to make them easier and faster to untie.

The author's favorite for all-around use and effectiveness. Ideal for securing loads that require a good deal of tension, the Trucker's Hitch includes a 3-to-1 mechanical advantage and is ideal for securing loads to vehicle rooftops. Use whenever tension is needed.

A mainstay of the nautical world and used for tying lines to sails, the Bowline is famous for staying tied. It is used to make a fixed loop in the end of a single line or join two ropes together with loops, attach lines to sails, or when a tether is needed.

A simple, effective knot for hanging or holding things, the Clove Hitch is traditional but useful today.

Perfect for joining two lines, and even lines of different diameter, the Fisherman's Knot is a fast, safe way to tie two ropes together.

The Double Figure Eight Loop is a strong knot that features an easily adjustable loop that is great for use in everything from monofilament to climbing ropes.

Perfect for tying small tackle and for hanging decorations, the Clinch Knot is a simple, fast favorite for tying monofilament fishing line.

The Basics

Knot Sense: A Simple Approach to Tying

Tying has been around for a long time, and over time, people have developed thousands of knots; most knot books include hundreds of different knots and instructions full of technical terms and complicated vocabulary. For the beginner, this can be overwhelming. What we really need is a simple, dependable approach to tying.

My book is different. I've included six simple knots that are easy to learn, useful, and simple to remember. The average person doesn't need a hundred knots for everyday, around-the-house tying. In all likelihood, they only need a handful. I'm confident my six will do the trick in almost any situation. So stay with these six knots!

You may not find your current favorites here, but the knots in this book will soon be among your favorites. Of course, some readers may feel other knots are superior to these six knots. If you know a better knot, by all means use it. You may simply add these to those you already know. And if after learning my knots you feel the need to learn more knots, please, don't let me stop you. For those of you who are really fired up to learn more, I've added a recommended reading page in the book. I applaud your knowledge. But this book is for beginners, for the knot novice, for those scared off by other knot-tying books. My goal is to help those in need of basic Knot Sense to quickly learn a small arsenal of knots, and how and when to use them. Afterwards, many of you will say these six knots are all you need to know.

The Only Assumptions I'm Making

I'm writing this book for beginners, and I'm not assuming you know a great deal about tying or that you even know how to tie a Square Knot. I'm also throwing the standard knot-tying lingo out the door. I've found that using technical terms only confuses the beginner. I'm striving for simplicity here, and I've done my best to write clear, simple instructions that correspond exactly to the how-to photographs. In fact, the only thing I'm assuming is that you know how to tie your shoes.

Interestingly, tying your shoes actually involves two basic steps of tying. The first, called the single overhand knot, is the first step in tying your shoelace. I also assume that all readers understand the granny knot. It is simply two single overhands tied one on top of the

other. After the first single overhand is tied, you simply tie another single overhand directly on top of it and then pull it tight. (Right over left, and then right over left again.) The granny knot is commonly tied, but it has flaws. You can do better, and I'll show you how.

How Knots Work—Pressure, Tension, Friction

First, it's important to understand how knots work. Generally, when we tie things, our objective is to help restrain or control the object. But before this is possible, one must overcome the internal tension of the rope itself; each line, rope, or string has its own degree of internal tension and resists bending to a certain extent. You've probably noticed this on your own. Really thick ropes are hard to tie because they have a good deal of internal tension, whereas string is easy to tie, as there is so little resistance.

Knots overcome this internal tension because of the combination of three forces: constant external tension, pressure, and friction. Constant tension occurs when ropes, wires, lines, or strings are continuously pulled to some degree of tightness. For instance, when one tunes a stringed instrument (a violin, for example), one is really adjusting the tension of the string to a desired level, then securing the string so it remains at that level of tension. It is that constant, yet adjustable, tension that can make such beautiful music in the tying process too!

Constant external tension generates pressure in the knot. This pressure compresses the individual threads of the rope (the weaves), which causes them to conform together. This, in turn, generates friction on the exterior surface

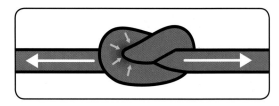

of the line, and the knot material latches together and stays tied, overcoming the internal resistance of the rope material. So, in almost all cases, a tight knot works better than a loose knot, as a tightly tied knot will create an adequate amount of external tension, pressure, and friction.

In some tying circumstances, however, it's not possible to have a constant external tension. When you're tying a tether, for instance, there is intermittent tension. Tension occurs only when the tethered animal or object moves or attempts to get free of the leash or line. That intermittent tension can sometimes coax knots loose, but some knots, like the Bowline, don't need constant tension. So be sure to use knots like the Bowline in these circumstances.

Use Specialized Knots When Needed

Now don't get me wrong, I'm not suggesting that my six knots are perfect for everything. Knot-tying is a perfect instance of the adage, "Necessity is the mother of invention." Specialized knots are the offspring of specialized needs. Always err on the side of safety. If you are going climbing, always learn climbing knots; if you're going sailing, learn sailing knots, and so on. With that said, there's no reason to use a complicated, technical knot when a simple one will do. More often than not, a simple knot will work just as well (or better).

Why Knots Fail

Sometimes, knots fail. Knots fail for two main reasons. First, knots fail if they are improperly tied. That's why it is so essential to learn how to tie knots correctly. Practice makes perfect. Second, knots fail when the wrong knot for the job is used. Oftentimes, people tend to tie one or two knots because they can remember them, and these knots sometimes work. Consequently, they try to make these one or two knots work in all situations. And even though these knots sometimes fail, people keep

using them because these knots are all they know. This lack of options often results in a disaster that could've been avoided with a little Knot Sense. So, it's important to use the right knot for the job, and to tie it properly.

Throughout the course of the book, I'll suggest a variety of uses for each knot, and photographs will show these knots in use in everyday, around-the-house tying situations. This way, you'll be able to avoid some of the trial-and-error that comes with learning how to tie, and you'll be able to avoid the trouble and inconvenience that comes with knots that have failed.

Knots are Finishing Tools

Before you go out and start tying, keep in mind that knots are finishing tools. There are other factors that can lead to knot-tying success or failure. For example, the quality of your rope is just as important as how well you tie your knots. If your rope is old, mildewed, and weak, it doesn't matter whether you tie the perfect

Bowline knot. If that's the case, your rope might snap and your boat may drift away from the dock, perfect Bowline and all. Similarly, if your car top carrier isn't attached properly, your kayak may stay tied to it, but both kayak and carrier might fly off if you hit the brakes.

The same goes for tying down objects that are liable to slide or slip. If you're tying a canoe directly to the roof of your car, you might need to introduce a stabilizing mechanism like a foam pad between car and canoe to augment the tension created by the knots and your rope. This will create enough friction to hold the canoe in place. If not,

your canoe might slip, causing the ropes to loosen or break, and your canoe might also go flying.

Of course, some people think that tying lots of knots is an alternative to learning how to tie, as shown in the photo to the left. I've heard the expression, "When you can't tie knots tie lots!" Unfortunately, this almost never works. Even if such knots work, it is almost always a waste of time and material, and doing so creates a knot that is always more difficult to untie. So my suggestion is simple: don't tie more knots—tie them right!

Knot Etiquette

Over the years, I have been a crew member aboard a variety of small boats (15' to 60'), including sailing vessels and powered vessels, and during such times I've found a little Knot Etiquette is sometimes called for aboard someone else's ship. That is to say, the skipper is in charge of the boat and may have a favorite knot or knots, so use them. Plus, standardized use of knots aboard a vessel is a great safety precaution because the crew always knows how to tie or untie them in

an emergency. In such cases, it's best for you to learn the skipper's knots and use them while aboard the ship. But don't worry, 99 percent of captains will be pleased that you know the Bowline.

I have also had great fun introducing several skippers to a few of the *Six Knots for Everyday Life*. I've left my mark on many vessels, because it is difficult to find a simpler, quicker approach to tying than my six knots. However, I hasten to add that a little Knot Etiquette is better than an argument on the boat when you are aboard as a guest! Then again, don't be afraid to mention a better knot if circumstances arise that warrant its use. I know more than one skipper who's lost a dinghy off the stern of the boat because of the manner in which it was tied. Once I

improperly tied dinghy

even lost my own! I even know of one skipper who lost his dinghy twice in the same day! His name will remain my secret. Passing on your knowledge of these six knots to prevent the loss of a dinghy would be well within the parameters of Knot Etiquette.

USE A SQUARE KNOT FOR TYING:

- Two ends of the same piece of string
- A decorative knot for scarves, belts, or other fashions
- Camping and hiking gear
- Packages and parcels
- In macrame and crafting
- Shoelaces
- In chores around the house

The Square Knot

The Square Knot gets a bum rap in some knot books, which suggest it *inadvertently comes untied*. I've never had one come untied, so I'd wager the "Square Knots" that failed were either tied improperly—as inadvertent Grannies or without proper tension—or used for the wrong purpose, as splices (which tie together two ropes) rather than knots. In any case, the blame for such failures lies not with the knot but with the person who tied it. Trust me, when used properly, the Square Knot is a good knot.

It's also easy to use and remember. In my experience, it's faster and easier to tie the Square Knot than the Bowline—a knot we'll soon discuss—and just as easy and quick to untie, especially when it's slipped.

Because of its simplicity, it has many uses, and is particularly useful around the house and in the yard. This certainly has something to do with its traditional popularity; in fact, the Boy Scouts have taught this knot for a long time. The best part is, it doesn't take long to learn. So what are you waiting for?

ADVANTAGES
- Easy to tie and untie
- Has many practical uses
- Lies flat when tied with cloth, making it ideal for bandages

TYING THE SQUARE KNOT

Okay, remember how to tie a Granny? The first steps in tying a Square Knot are exactly like a Granny. Just remember, right over left, then left over right.

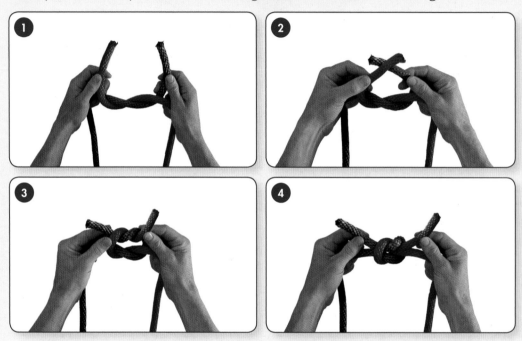

1. Cross the right end of the line (red) over the left end of the line (blue). Bring the right end under the line and back up.

2. Cross the right end (red) over the left end (blue) again, forming another loop.

3. Tuck the right end (red) under the line and pull it back up.

4. Pull on all four lines to tighten and to center the knot.

Variations

TYING A SLIPPED SQUARE KNOT

A Slipped Square Knot is easy to tie and quicker to untie than a non-slipped Square Knot. To tie a Slipped Square Knot, begin with plenty of rope on the left side with which to form a loop, then:

1. Complete step 1 of the regular Square Knot, then form a large loop in the left end of the rope (dark) on the left side of the knot.

2. Lay the loop over the right end (light), then tuck it back underneath.

3. Tighten the knot by pulling on the loop and the right end (light).

LOCKING A SQUARE KNOT

A Square Knot, even when slipped, can be further secured by tying a Half-Hitch in each working end of the knot.

1. Complete regular Square Knot steps 1-4, then take the right end (dark) of rope on the right side of the knot and cross it over the line.

2. Pass the right end (dark) under the line and through the loop.

3. Tighten the knot by pulling on the right end (dark).

4. These steps can also be completed on the opposite side of the knot to secure that end as well.

Tips

HELPFUL HINTS

The Square Knot performs best if it is tied under tension, so between steps 3 and 4, keep the ends taut by using one of the following methods:

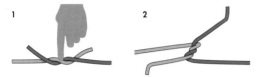

1. Have someone hold their thumb or finger on that first tie

2. If no one is around to help, twist the lines 180 degrees to pinch the tension in place in that first overhand knot, then tie the left-over-right knot by jerking it tight with both hands

DO

- Tie it with pressure, under tension
- Remember: right over left, then left over right
- Use it when securing the end of a line that will remain under tension

DON'T

- Use it for monofilament fishing line, because it will slip
- Use it to tie two ropes together (splice), as it can easily come undone
- Tie a Granny by mistake
- Use the Square Knot if another knot is better suited to the task at hand

MATERIALS

Square Knots work well with cloths such as scarves and linens. In addition, they work well with most fiber ropes but fare poorly with stiff or slippery rope, or monofilament. No tying aids are required, unless you have a friend volunteer to hold their finger on the knot.

FUN FACTS

The Square Knot is also known as the Reef Knot, for its use tying reefs—parts of sails that are folded or rolled up before a storm. Clipper ships reefed their sails with Square Knots because they were easy to tie and untie. It has been around for thousands of years, dating back to ancient Greece, Rome and Egypt. The Romans called it the Hercules Knot and Greek brides tied their belts with a Square Knot in the hope it would make them fertile.

USE A SLIP KNOT FOR TYING:

- Tying a car trunk shut
- Fly-fishing equipment
- Tarps, tents, and other shelters
- Plastic trash or storage bags
- Hanging food while camping
- Securing tent poles
- Projects around the house
- Camping gear

②

The Slip Knot

A Slip Knot sometimes seems more like a way of finishing a knot than a knot itself, but it is a highly useful knot in its own right. In fact, the Slip Knot is my first choice because it is such a great knot for practical, everyday tying. It is simple, efficient, universally adaptable, and takes almost no time to tie or untie.

The Slip Knot is also useful in concert with many other knots, as they can be *slipped*, which transfers the Slip Knot's *quick untie* characteristics to other knots. With that said, I must note that when it is used improperly it can be a dangerous knot, because it is so easy to untie. In order to avoid a potentially dangerous situation, make sure you learn (and use) the specialized knots for activities such as climbing, caving, and the like.

But don't let that scare you off. For around-the-house use, the Slip Knot is great. You won't find a knot that's more handy, simpler to learn, or quicker to tie or untie.

ADVANTAGES

- Easiest to tie and untie
- Adaptable to many uses
- Can be incorporated into other knots to make them easier to untie
- One of the easiest knots to tie without losing tension in the line

TYING THE SLIP KNOT
Tying a Slip Knot by Itself:

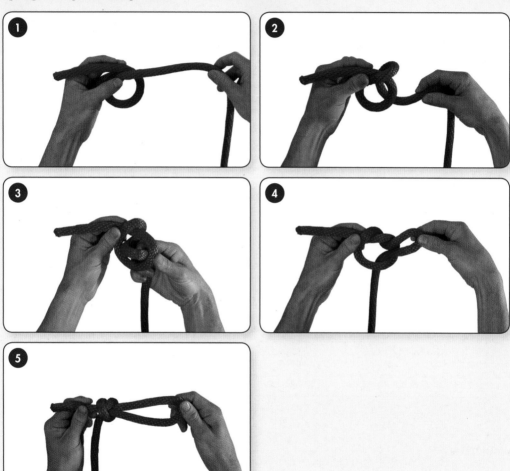

1. Cross the right end behind and over the line, so the right end is on top. Pull the right end forward a few inches.

2. Twist the right end and begin to push it through the loop.

3. Keep pushing until a section of the right end is through the loop.

4. Reach through the loop and grab the right end of the line. Pull it through the loop until tight. Now you can adjust the placement of the knot by pulling on either end.

5. You can make the loop larger or smaller by sliding the line through the knot (before pulling it tight).

Tying a Slip Knot Around Something:

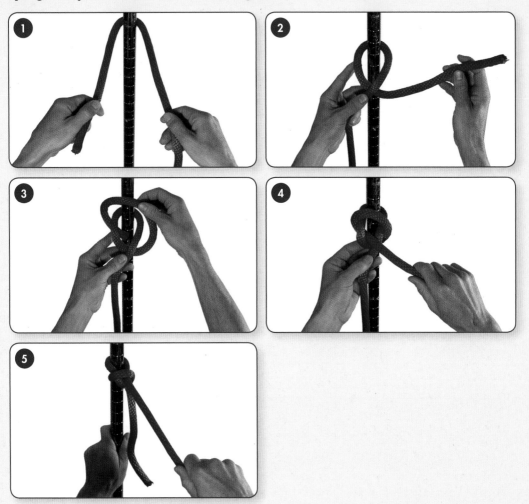

The Slip Knot

1. Loop the rope around the object once, leaving the left end in your left hand.

2. Bring the left end under the right end. This creates a loop.

3. Bring the left end over itself and then through the loop.

4. Pull the left end through the loop.

5. Continue pulling to tighten and pull the left end to loosen the knot.

Variations
LOCKING A SLIP KNOT

1. Lengthen the loop if necessary.
2. Loop the end of the line around the line above the knot.
3. Pull the line back through the opening you just created.
4. This knot does not have to be tightly cinched, and is easier to untie if left loose.

Tips
HELPFUL HINTS

DO
- Lock a Slip Knot to prevent it from coming untied

DON'T
- Use a Slip Knot with large-diameter lines
- Use a Slip Knot for specialized tasks that call for other specialized knots, like climbing or sailing

FUN FACTS

I think it's safe to say that the Slip Knot is one of the most tied knots in the world. After all, the ubiquitous bow used to secure shoelaces everywhere is actually a Double Slip Knot (two Slip Knots tied with a single Overhand Knot).

USE A TRUCKER'S HITCH TO:

- Secure loads on trailers or vehicles
- Tie down a tarp
- Tie objects that require tension
- Tie a canoe to your car top
- Carry lumber on a roof rack
- Tow heavy loads
- Tie a tent or tarp

The Trucker's Hitch

The Trucker's Hitch is one of my favorite knots. While it looks complex, the Trucker's Hitch is actually quite simple and is nothing more than a pair of strategically placed Slip Knots. This ingenious combination creates a 3-to-1 mechanical advantage, as the two Slip Knots form a pulley. The first Slip Knot is the "Pulley Loop" and makes it easy to apply a good deal of tension to a line, whereas the second Slip Knot locks the desired amount of tension into the line.

The Trucker's Hitch is also one of the easiest knots to tie, adjust, and untie because it utilizes Slip Knots. The real beauty is its versatility and adaptability. It can be configured to suit nearly any need, and this makes it one of the handiest knots to know. I will add here, before someone else does, that you can also use the Bowline to form the "Pulley Loop," but to me it's more work that way. Slip Knots have worked for me with the Trucker's Hitch all these years.

In short, the Trucker's Hitch combines maximum leverage and tension with ultimate simplicity. Have I mentioned that I love this knot? You will, too!

ADVANTAGES

- Non-jamming
- Works like a pulley, offering a 3-to-1 mechanical advantage
- Fun and easy to tie quickly

TYING THE TRUCKER'S HITCH

Note: This knot starts with one end of the rope tied to a support and the other end of the rope draped over the object you want to secure.

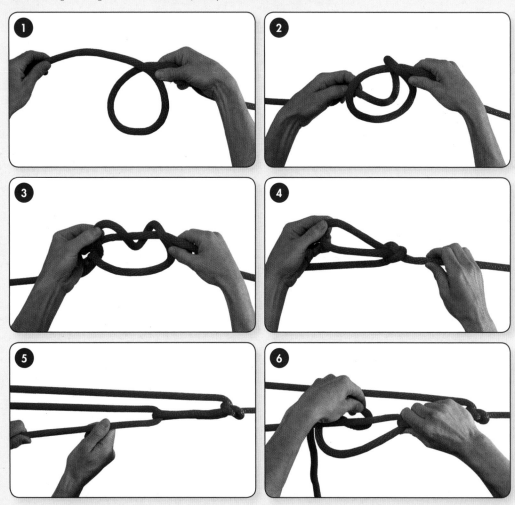

1. Create a loop in the middle of the rope with your right hand.

2. With your left hand, pull a section of the rope on your left through the loop.

3. Pull this section through the loop and upward with your left hand. This creates another loop.

4. Pull this loop to tighten. This creates the first slip knot (the "Pulley Loop").

5. Wrap the remaining line around the other support and bring the remainder of the line through the Pulley Loop. Pull the end down to tighten; you can tighten as much as you wish.

6. Pinch the free end and the slip knot loop with your right hand. Create a loop in the remaining free line.

7. Wrap the loop around the lines you're pinching. This creates another loop. Pass the loop in your left hand through the center. This is another slip knot.

8. Pull the loop tight before releasing the lines. This way you don't lose any tension.

Variations

LOCKING A TRUCKER'S HITCH

The Trucker's Hitch can be secured by tying a half-hitch in the slipped loop above the second Slip Knot.

1. Wrap the second slip knot over the bottom line.
2. Bring the line under and back up.
3. This creates another loop.
4. Thread the second slip knot through the loop and pull it tight.

Tips

HELPFUL HINTS

The first Slip Knot (the "Pulley Loop") can be placed wherever you want it to be, and you can apply whatever degree of tension you want and are only constrained by the breaking strength of the rope you're working with. The size of the second Slip Knot's loop can also be adjusted by simply pulling on the tail of the loop (to make it smaller), or on the loop itself (to make it larger). This ease of adjustment enables you to make the loop large enough to add a half-hitch.

DO

- Snug the knot down tight
- Tie it with tension on the line to hold the load securely

DON'T

- Overtighten beyond the line's break strength
- Tie the knot repeatedly in the same place in the line, as this can cause the rope to fray

MATERIALS

The Trucker's Hitch can be used with a wide variety of line diameters and materials. I have used it with thread for dainty jobs, and with bulky tow rope—pulling on the Pulley Loop with a pickup truck—to move a large object over the ground. It works best with lines not much larger than 1 inch in diameter—and performs even better with thinner lines.

FUN FACTS

The Trucker's Hitch has been around at least since the days of ox carts and horse-drawn carriages, and people have long enjoyed its usefulness and simplicity. It is also known as the Lorry Hitch, Haymaker's Hitch, Harvester's Hitch and the Dolly Knot.

wheelbarrow tied to a trailer

USE A BOWLINE FOR TYING:

- Sails or lines on a ship
- Tethers for a horse or dog
- Mooring lines to a canoe or kayak
- Camping gear
- A hammock or tire swing

The Bowline

Long used at sea, the Bowline (pronounced *boh-linn*) has many handy applications at home and elsewhere ashore. It's particularly useful as it creates a fixed loop, and can therefore be adapted to many household uses. In addition, the Bowline is famous for staying tied, and is one of the most dependable knots I know.

With that said, some knot books and online resources speak a little disparagingly about the Bowline, suggesting that it can fail in certain circumstances. However, over the years, I've used the Bowline often and it has been very reliable, so I'm willing to bet the Bowlines that failed weren't tied correctly. The Bowline's a good knot; if you tie it correctly, it'll work.

ADVANTAGES
- Easy to tie
- Does not slip
- Stays tied

TYING THE BOWLINE

This knot is usually used to make a loop.

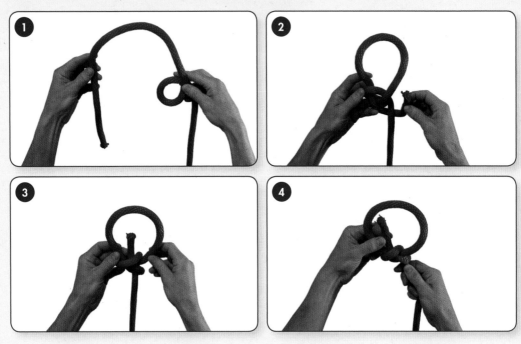

1. Form a small loop over the line in your right hand.

2. Thread the line through the loop and behind the rest of the line.

3. Pass the line back up through the original loop.

4. Tighten by pulling on the rest of the line.

Variations

TYING A SLIPPED BOWLINE

Like any slipped knot, a Slipped Bowline is easier to untie than a non-slipped Bowline.

To tie a Slipped Bowline, start with a little extra rope—say, 18 inches—on the working end so you have plenty with which to form a loop and tie the knot, then:

1. Follow steps 1 and 2 for a Bowline by forming a small loop over the line, then feeding the end up through the loop and beneath the rest of the line.

2. Form a larger loop (roughly 7 inches long) in the end of the line.

3. Push this loop down through the original loop, taking care not to twist the loop in the process (which can make it more difficult to untie the knot).

4. Tighten the knot tight by pulling on the ends of the line.

LOCKING A BOWLINE

For added security, a Bowline can be locked by tying a Half-Hitch in the tail of the knot.

1. Complete the regular Bowline steps 1–4.

2. Pass the end of the rope over the right side of the loop.

3. Tuck it under the rope and back through the small loop you just created.

4. Snug the resulting Half-Hitch tight to secure the knot.

Tips

DO

- Use the Bowline for tethering pets and attaching a line to something under intermittent tension

- Use this knot when you cannot tie with constant tension and the resulting pressure and friction

DON'T

- Tie it with slippery rope

- Use it under tension when other knots will do a better job; I recommend the Trucker's Hitch for tying under tension

- Use it in situations where the line will be working back and forth against the knot (unless you lock it with a Half-Hitch)

FUN FACTS

The Bowline is an old knot that dates back at least to the fifteenth century. It is named for the "bow line," a sailing term that describes the rope used to secure the edge of a square sail toward the ship's bow (and into the wind). To this day, the Bowline is likely the most respected knot in the nautical world, and in my opinion, one of the most useful knots on a boat.

USE A CLOVE HITCH FOR TYING:

- Tethers for a horse or dog
- Mooring lines
- Ornaments around the house
- Stakes or trees in the garden
- Lashings
- Tarps and tents
- While hiking
- Lines along a series of posts

The Clove Hitch

The Clove Hitch is one of the simplest and most versatile of knots, consisting of little more than two Half-Hitches. It can be tied around stakes, posts, trees or similar objects, tossed loosely over the top of a vertical post, and used in a variety of other handy ways.

I learned it as a kid, from fishermen who used it to tie their herring skiffs to dock posts. One of the best things about the Clove Hitch is, the harder you pull on it, the tighter it gets—and it tends to remain tight, even without tension. It can be locked with an extra Half-Hitch, or finished with a Slip Knot for fast untying.

ADVANTAGES
- Easy to tie
- Many practical uses

TYING THE CLOVE HITCH
Tying a Vertical Clove Hitch:

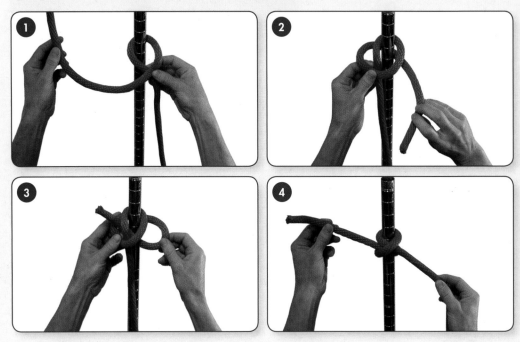

1. With the rope in your left hand, cross over line, creating a loop. Place this loop over the vertical bar or peg.

2. Take the end of the line and wrap it clockwise around the vertical bar.

3. Then take the end of the line and sneak it between itself and the rest of the line.

4. Pull through to tighten.

Tying a Horizontal Clove Hitch:

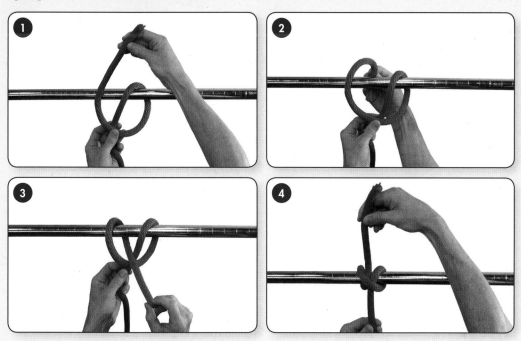

1. Wrap the line over the bar and back up.

2. Then bring the end over the bar again.

3. Bring the end under the bar and pull straight toward you.

4. Then bring the end straight up and pull tight on it, and the rest of the line, to tighten.

Variations

TYING A SLIPPED CLOVE HITCH

Like any slipped knot, a Slipped Clove Hitch is easier to untie than a non-slipped Clove Hitch. It is best used for brief, temporary tying. To tie a Slipped Clove Hitch, start with a little extra rope on the working end so you have plenty with which to form a loop and tie the knot, then:

1. Follow steps 1-3 for tying a regular Clove Hitch. Form a loop in the free end of the line.

2. Bring the loop beneath the second wrap.

3. Tighten the knot by pulling on the loop and rest of the line.

LOCKING A CLOVE HITCH

For added security, most people simply tie another wrap in the Clove Hitch, but occasionally it is easier to use a Half-Hitch—such as when the line is tied around a large-diameter object and it would use up too much line to add a third wrap.

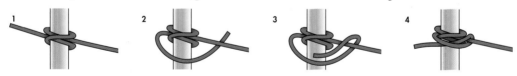

1. Complete Clove Hitch steps 1-4.

2. Pass the end of the rope over the rest of the line.

3. Tuck the line under the rope and back through the small loop you just created.

4. Snug the resulting Half-Hitch tight to secure the knot.

TYING A 3-WRAP CLOVE HITCH

A friend of mine teaches people the 3-wrap Clove Hitch in this manner:

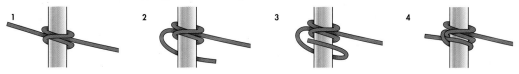

1. Complete Clove Hitch steps 1-4.
2. Loop the line from left to right around the post.
3. Bring the line around and below the first wrap.
4. Pull the end through the resulting loop to tighten.

Tips

To really learn the Clove Hitch, try making 10 wraps in a row! This exercise will be helpful as you attempt to use the Clove Hitch in different situations.

DO

- Add a third wrap or Half-Hitch when tying the Clove Hitch around a smooth surface
- Use this knot when you cannot tie with tension, pressure and friction

DON'T

- Use it on objects that can turn or it may unroll under high tension

FUN FACTS

Also referred to as the Builder's Knot or Builder's Hitch, the Clove Hitch was used on ships to fasten ratlines to shrouds—forming the rope ladders you see sailors scrambling up in the movies.

USE A FISHERMAN'S KNOT/GRANNY SPLICE FOR TYING:

- Lines of different diameters together
- Short lines together to form a long rope
- While fishing
- While kayaking or canoeing
- Towlines
- Jewelry, especially necklaces
- Inner tubes or waterskiing lines

The Fisherman's Knot
OR Granny Splice

I learned this knot from a commercial fisherman in Grand Marais, Minnesota. He called it the Granny Splice. Whatever you call it, it is the quickest, simplest, easiest way I know to join two or more lines together.

Ingenious in its simplicity, the Fisherman's Knot is made up of two single overhand knots pulled against each other. The combination always stays tied—in fact, the splice becomes tighter the harder you pull on it.

Though simple, this knot is extremely handy. Once, on a canoe trip, I used the Fisherman's Knot to bind five different short lines into one to create a rope long enough to help me line my canoe through a rapids, rather than portage.

ADVANTAGES

- There is no easier or more effective method of making a long line out of two or more short ones

- It works with ropes of different diameter, if under tension

TYING THE FISHERMAN'S KNOT

Note: This knot is easier to tie with the lines in your lap.

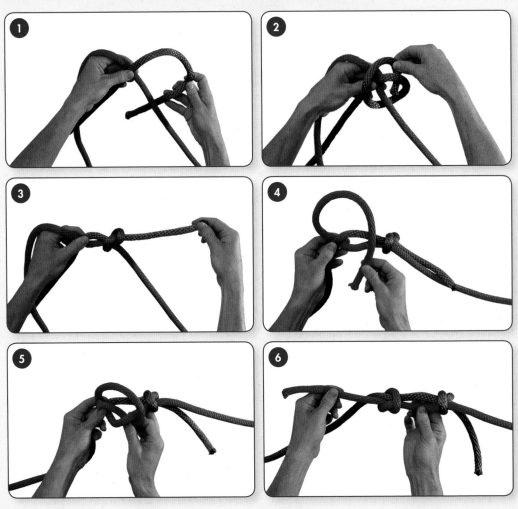

The Fisherman's Knot/Granny Splice

1. Begin with the two ropes parallel to each other, then cross the ends.

2. Bring the blue line under the red line; then bring the blue line up and over itself to form a loop. Tuck the end of the blue line under to form an overhand knot.

3. Pull the blue line tight.

4. Now, do the same thing for the red line. Bring the red end over the blue line, making sure to go around both lines.

5. Bring the red end through the loop.

6 Pull the red end tight.

7. Now grasp the blue line and the red line and pull the lines away from one another. This will cause the knots to slide together.

8. Pull the ropes until tight. The knots will block one another and hold the ropes together. Be sure to leave the ends of the knot long enough to grasp. This makes it easier to untie.

Variations

TYING A SLIPPED FISHERMAN'S KNOT

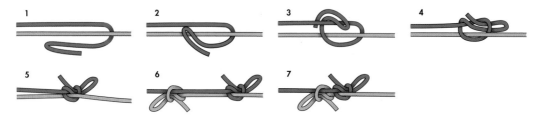

1. Place the lines parallel to each other, and place the top line under the bottom line.

2. Form a loop in the end of the top line.

3. Bring the loop between the two lines and over. This creates a loop.

4. Bring the end of the line through the opening.

5. Pull the loop through until tightened. The resulting knot will have a free end and a loop as shown.

6. Repeat the process with the bottom line.

7. Pull the lines in opposite directions to slide the knots together.

LOCKING A GRANNY SPLICE

I have never found it necessary to lock a Granny Splice. But if it will make you feel safer, you can lock the splice by hitching the free ends around the line.

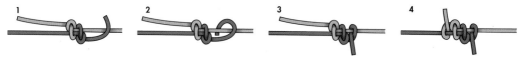

1. Take the end of the knot on the right and wrap it over the top line.

2. Bring the line over and back under the line. This creates a small loop.

3. Bring the end through the small loop.

4. Pull tight. Repeat on the other half of the knot.

Tips

HELPFUL HINTS

If you're using rope more than ½ inch in diameter, a Fisherman's Knot may come untied if there is no tension on the lines. However, as long as the knots are tight and there is pressure holding them together, the splice will not fail no matter the size of the ropes.

DO

- To untie a Granny Splice, start by pulling the tails of the knots in opposite directions; this will slide the knots apart
- Use a double-hitched Granny Splice to tie a necklace or lanyard; because the splice is adjustable (by sliding the knots together or apart), you can easily lengthen or shorten it

DON'T

- Use rope larger than ½ inch if the splice will not be kept under tension

FUN FACTS

The Granny Splice is most often known as the Fisherman's Knot. Though it is sometimes also called the True Lovers' Knot for its symmetry—the actual True Lovers' Knot involves two Overhand Knots tied together. Whatever you call it, the Granny Splice is easy to tie and effective. It can actually save you when you need a long line but have only short ropes.

USE THE BONUS KNOTS TO TIE:

- A fixed loop in the end of the line
- Large fishing tackle like Rapalas, shad raps, and crankbaits
- Ornaments and decorations around the house
- While climbing
- Smaller fishing tackle, leaders, and other gear
- While caving
- Camping gear, tents, and equipment

Bonus Knots

Monofilament fishing line is very popular among fishermen; however, its hardness and slipperiness cause otherwise reliable knots to slip and fail. Specialized knots are required for monofilament, and this often scares many folks away from it. This is a real shame, because monofilament line isn't just for fishing. In fact, it has many uses around the house as well.

While a number of special fishing knots will hold monofilament line, the Double Figure Eight Loop and the Clinch Knot are the simplest, quickest, and easiest-to-tie monofilament knots that I know. Together, these two knots will cover all of your fishing needs, and you'll find them extremely useful around the house. For instance, many people use monofilament to hang decorations, such as mistletoe, and the like because monofilament is practically invisible.

And if you're planning on using these knots for fishing, you're all set. The Double Figure Eight Loop is best suited to large fishing tackle (and can be used with a variety of different ropes as well), whereas I'd recommend the Clinch Knot for smaller tackle.

ADVANTAGES

- Easy to tie and untie
- Offer a fast and easy way to switch lures when fishing
- Do not slip
- Loop size is adjustable

TYING THE DOUBLE FIGURE EIGHT LOOP

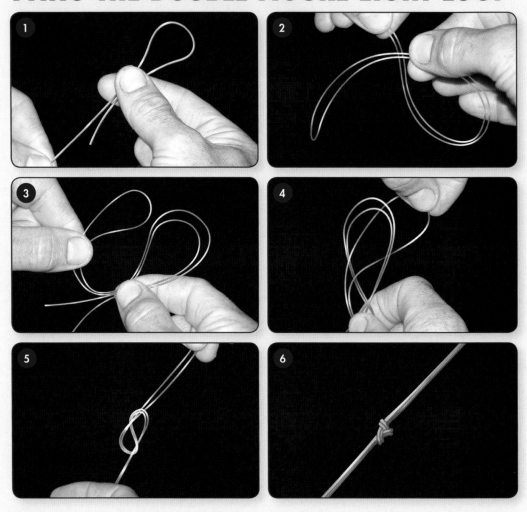

BONUS KNOTS: The Double Figure Eight Loop and The Clinch Knot

1. Make a loop by doubling a section of line.

2. Cross the loop back over itself.

3. Bring it under and around the line.

4. Pass it down through the loop.

5. Tighten the knot by pulling the loop (in one hand) and the end of the line in opposite directions.

6. The completed knot looks just like a figure eight pattern.

ATTACHING IT TO SOMETHING

Once the Double Figure Eight Loop is pulled tight, you can attach it to ornaments, fishing lures, and other items in one of two simple ways.

1. Thread the loop through the eye.
2. Pass the object back through the loop.
3. Pull the knot tight at the point of attachment.

Tips
HELPFUL HINTS

The length of the loop is the key to using this knot. When hanging ornaments, keep the loop short to decrease visibility. With lures, the loop must be a little longer than the lure to be threaded through it.

DO

- Use a small scissors or nail clipper to trim excess line from the tail of the knot
- Moisten the line with water or saliva before tightening the knot

DON'T

- Reuse a section of monofilament line if becomes nicked (which weakens it); check for damage by running the line between your thumb and forefinger

FUN FACTS

Although the Double Figure Eight Loop is a great choice for monofilament, it also works well with many types of rope. Sometimes called the Figure Eight Loop, it's used for a variety of everyday purposes and even for fishing and sailing. Some even use it in place of the Bowline because, though it is not as easy to untie, it's less likely to be improperly tied.

TYING THE CLINCH KNOT

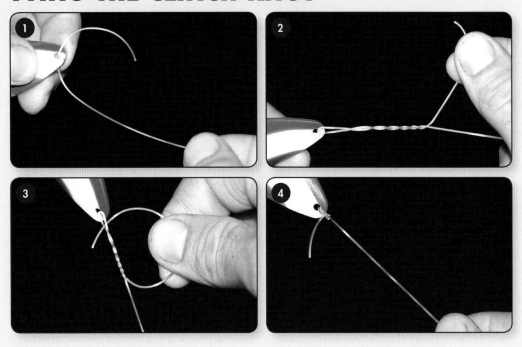

1. Insert the line through the eyelet on the end of the tackle or ornament.

2. Pull the line through and twist it around the line five or six times.

3. Take the end of the line and bring it back through the loop near the eyelet on the end of the tackle or ornament.

4. Grasp the object you're tying to with your left hand and the long line with your right. Pull them apart until tight. Cut off the tag end of the line.

A favorite of fly fishermen, its main purpose is to attach swivels, hooks and lures to the primary fishing line. When fishing, I always use the Double Figure Eight Knot when tying to large lures, and the Clinch Knot when using small ones. This knot is good for small fishing lures because it stays tied, it doesn't weaken monofilament line (as traditional knots tend to do), and it is one of the smaller fishing knots, so it doesn't create a disturbance when tied to a lure and tossed in the water, which a bigger knot might do. There are many, many more knots out there for tying monofilament and exotic fishing lines. If you're feeling ambitious or are eager for more, give them a try. In the meantime, the simple Clinch Knot shown here will do the trick.

Tips

HELPFUL HINTS

You can use the Clinch Knot to hang decorations too! People like to use monofilament line because it is nearly invisible; unlike other tying materials, it allows you to hang things so they appear to be floating in air because you cannot easily see the line.

DO

- Use the Clinch Knot for fishing and for home decoration. I know of no fisherman who ever lost a lure with this knot or had a Christmas tree ornament fall off the tree!

DON'T

- Forget to cut off the tag end of the line when you're finished. If you don't, this could distract the fish or cause houseguests to notice how you hung your ornaments.

FUN FACTS

The Clinch Knot is also known as the Half Blood Knot and the Stevedore's Knot. Interestingly, there isn't a lot of written history about the Clinch Knot. The one bit that's out there has to do with the Clinch Knot's name; historians have often argued about how the Clinch Knot got its name. No matter what the knot is called, it has been in use for a long time. But for most of its history, it was not used in monofilament line, as monofilament has only existed for 50 years or so.

IN THIS CHAPTER, WE'LL DISCUSS:

- Car top carriers and car racks
- Foam pads and other protective gear
- Tying with loops
- Types of ropes
- Tying scenarios
- Harnessing
- How to tie a load to your car
- Tying questions and answers
- How to lock and secure knots

Tying Aids

Tying Aids and Materials

There are many different types of rope out there, and a good deal of equipment that can make tying with ropes easier, safer, and more reliable. But don't think you have to rush out and buy everything in sight. I'm here to act as your guide.

The Right Stuff

First, we'll start with ropes. There are many kinds of rope. Traditionally, ropes were made of organic fibers—hemp, cotton, and the like. Nowadays, rope is more often than not made of synthetic fibers like nylon, polyester, or polypropylene and even out of exotic materials like Kevlar (the same material used for bullet-proof vests). Each type of rope has benefits and drawbacks. Synthetic ropes are much stronger than natural ropes and are more resistant to mildew and aging. But organic ropes are cheaper and generally have a fairly respectable breaking strength.

In addition, some ropes are useful for specific circumstances; for instance, polypropylene ropes often float and are useful on the water, and certain ropes are brightly colored for use in low-light conditions. My favorites tend to be synthetics, especially nylons, because they resist deterioration, and their internal tension and surface textures make them easy to tie.

In any case, before purchasing a rope, be sure to check its break strength, find out what it is made of (which is usually listed on the package), and check out your old ropes before using them to make sure they are in good condition. Rope age, fraying, and other factors can reduce break strength by a considerable margin. Again, be sure to err on the side of safety.

Racks, Car Toppers, and Carriers

Aside from rope, there are many other pieces of equipment that you might find useful, especially if you're planning on carrying gear on top of a vehicle. You've no

doubt seen this type of equipment before; everyone's familiar with car top kayak and canoe carriers, car top bike racks, and the like. Even though it's helpful, this type of equipment still often requires the use of ropes and other tying materials. In fact, most racks are designed with tying in mind; it's easy to tie things onto such racks/carriers or within them.

But some helpful gear might be less than obvious. People new to tying sometimes attempt to harness a load on a rooftop rack by using more ropes, different ropes, and additional wraps of the lines, which generally involves *more* tying instead of *better* tying. A better approach is to introduce the use of materials or pads between the item being carried and the rack itself. By placing a softer material, even a thin one, between the load and the rack, one can generate friction and resistance to movement between the

two hard surfaces. A thicker material is better still, especially something that will compress and conform to both surfaces. Many such pads are commercially available for purchase.

For instance, let's say you're going paddling. If you put a boat, canoe, or kayak directly on top of a car, this puts two hard, slippery and potentially unstable surfaces together. If there is sudden motion, the boat may slip or move, as there is little friction between the two surfaces. Each time the boat moves on the rack, this loosens the ropes. Continuous motion due to wind resistance compounds this problem, and could potentially lead to loosening of the harness and an unsafe situation.

An easy solution is to place a foam pad or cushion between the boat and the car top rack. A thick material, like the foam blocks shown, compresses and conforms to the shape and surface of the canoe and the car rack. Naturally a thicker block will compress and conform more than a thin block. Like the motor mounts of an automobile engine, the blocks act as shock absorbers. They accept the small 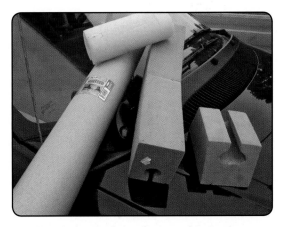 amounts of wobble caused by speed, wind, and braking without losing the friction generated by the surfaces against them. This works wonders, as it ensures there is friction and reduces instability. In addition, foam, pads and cushions prevent damage to both the boat and the car.

And when needed, padding can be easily and inexpensively invented with a little ingenuity. Almost any form of compressible material can be used in a pinch, with the idea that the more friction its surfaces generate, the better. I have used life jackets, children's foam tube toys, and a variety of rubber pieces, including chunks of folded tire inner tubes. In the end, it is not always about how good the padding looks, but rather how well it gets the job done. It is also important to select materials that will not absorb water if you are driving in the rain.

It makes sense to take advantage of available harnessing equipment like foam pads and car top carriers when they are available from stores around you. Then again, don't become dependent on such gear; you should know how to adequately tie without them in case equipment isn't available.

Tying with Loops

One of the easiest ways to tie a load to your car is to start with a line that has a loop affixed to its end. The easiest way to place a loop in the end of whatever you're tying is as follows: Bend the end of the line back parallel with the longer portion of the line. Grasp both pieces and simply tie a single overhand knot, making the length of the loop the desired size before pulling it tight.

Starting this way eliminates the need to create any kind of a knot to secure the first end of the line. For instance, if you are tying to a roof top rack with ends solidly attached to the car top, simply slip the loop beneath the rack and thread the other end of the line through it. Then you are ready to proceed with the tying task. Using loops in this manner also eliminates the need to untie a knot when you are finished.

In addition, you can use this technique in many other ways. For instance, you can suspend a variety of loads within a threaded-loop line. There often is no need to even tie it, because the weight suspended within the loop will keep it tight. A loop also works well to suspend something from above.

When tying, ropes can become snarled, and sometimes impossibly snarled. Using loops eliminates the need for a knot on one end of the line and therefore prevents lines from becoming needlessly tangled. Loops are particularly useful for these two reasons; they make it quicker and easier to tie and untie. In fact, a looped end works on almost anything you may need to tie to.

Tying a Load to Your Car

Use a common sense approach when tying a load to the roof of your vehicle. Think of the possibility of having to hit the brakes hard to avoid an accident. Though hitting the brakes saves you from an accident, your load sliding off the roof could easily cause another for which you would still be liable.

So tie the correct knot (a Trucker's Hitch is never a bad idea) and add additional lines for stability. For instance, when I tie my

canoe to the rack I always add a short tie from the forward thwart of the canoe directly to one of the cross bars of the roof rack. Even if I lock up the brakes that canoe is not going to leave the roof! That small piece of extra line is cheap insurance.

A stabilizing front and rear tie is a must with long loads like lumber or a canoe or kayak. This prevents the front and rear of the load (which has the greatest leverage) from pivoting around the center of the load. Allowing your load to wobble horizontally stretches and loosens the tie lines over time. The looser your load becomes the more apt you are to lose it due to wind or sudden braking. Dual bow and stern lines are most effective and don't cause too much downward pressure. I know many who never use front or rear stabilizing ties. I consider this unwise; at the least, a front tie to stabilize horizontal movement of a long load is a good idea. I can't say this enough: when in doubt, err on the side of caution.

Locking Knots With Half-Hitches

Sometimes a knot needs to be locked in place so it doesn't come untied inadvertently. An easy way to lock a knot is with a half-hitch. A half-hitch isn't really a knot. In fact, it's similar to a single overhand knot—a way of starting or finishing a knot—rather than a finished knot. Even so, you should know how to tie it, in case you need to lock

Locked Square Knot **Locked Slip Knot** **Locked Trucker's Hitch**

Locked Bowline **Locked Clove Hitch** **Locked Fisherman's Knot**

a knot. Tying it is easy. All you need to do is take the free end of the rope, cross it over the line (this creates a loop), and bring it back up through the loop and pull tight. All six knots in this book can be locked with a half-hitch.

A Slip Knot can be secured by tying a half-hitch in the slipped loop above the actual Slip Knot. A Square Knot can be secured by tying a half-hitch in each free tail of the knot. A Fisherman's Knot can be secured by tying a half-hitch in each free tail of the knots. A Trucker's Hitch can be secured by tying a half-hitch in the slipped loop above the actual Slip Knot. A Bowline can be further secured by tying a half-hitch in the free tail end of the Bowline. A Clove Hitch can be further secured by tying a half-hitch in the free tail end of the Clove Hitch.

Only you can decide when or when not to use half-hitches as extra security for the knots you use. It will be easier to decide as you become familiar with use of the six knots. Trust your instincts! Use half-hitches as you feel necessary.

Slipped Square Knot   **Slipped Clove Hitch**   **Slipped Fisherman's Knot**   **Slipped Bowline**

Slipping the Six

As previously stated, all of the *Six Knots for Everyday Life* can be slipped. Slipping any knot simply adds the quick untie characteristic of the Slip Knot to any knot you are working with, but be sure to secure knots you slip as the quick untie characteristic means the knots may come untied if you're not careful. Before you start tying, be sure to:

- Use materials strong enough for what you are tying
- Choose the simplest, most effective way of harnessing
- Choose the knot best suited to your tying task
- Use whatever tying aids are necessary
- Always err on the side of safety
- Think of untying as well; it's no fun wrestling with a knot that's hard to untie
- Use specialized knots when called for

These bits of advice and suggestions will become increasingly familiar to you as you use this book. They'll soon become second nature. And that's when your friends will begin to say, "How did you do that?"

Moving On

I hope many of you are motivated to learn more about tying than I could pack into this book. There are many, many books and thousands of knots to look over and utilize. New methods, new knots, and new materials are constantly appearing and I suspect always will be. With the kinds of material, configurations, and better mousetraps coming to the market, you should expect change.

In the meantime, use and teach these six knots to others. Don't let anyone you know go through life counting on only Velcro, duct tape, and wire. One can take pride in a good knot and in knowing how to use it. Every time I use a rope from my Possibles bag it makes me feel good. I remember when someone taught me this or that knot and the accomplishment I felt when it worked. I also remember how good that same knowledge makes others feel. I figure I'm getting too old to pass on much more, but I hope I have helped you along the way and that you will help someone else. That's how it has always worked . . . and that is how it's supposed to be!

About the Author

Phil Peterson Sr. grew up in Grand Marais, Minnesota, on Lake Superior, next to the Boundary Waters Canoe Area. He has explored that area summer and winter for most of his adult life. In addition he pursued a life of adventure sailing on a variety of boats and accruing some 30,000 miles of adventures, crossing oceans among them. He makes no claims to being a knot expert. He simply wants to pass on the practical knowledge of everyday utility tying he has accrued through his 70 plus years of harnessing his adventures. He says, "Why should people have to page through hundreds of knots when a half dozen will get them through life?"

Married for 45 years, Phil and his wife raised five interesting children into accomplished adults while working near and playing on the Great Lakes, Puget Sound, and oceans east and west. He also had a 50-year career in the U.S. ski industry.

Phil and his wife now live in the beautiful St. Croix River valley. He is an accomplished woodworker, builder of his own canoes and kayaks, a photo journalist, an average poet and author of more things to come with a focus on "continued adventures until the day I drop."

He can be contacted via email at callphil@ecenet.com

RECOMMENDED READING

Bigon, M. and Regazzoni, G., *The Morrow Guide to Knots*, New York: William Morrow and Company Publishing, 1981.

Jarman, Colin, *The Essential Knot Book: Knots, Bends, Hitches, Whippings, Splices*, 2nd edition, Camden, ME: International Marine Publishing, 2000.

Pawson, Des, *Handbook of Knots*, London: Dorling Kindersley Books, 2004.

Peterson, Sr., Phil, *All Things are Possible, The Verlen Kruger Story: 100,000 Miles by Paddle*, Cambridge, MN: Adventure Publications, 2006.

Smith, Garrett Hervey, *The Arts of the Sailor: Knotting, Splicing and Ropework*, Mineola, NY: Dover Publications, 1990.